HOTEL BRAVO

Alexandra Payne
HOTEL BRAVO

AN EYEWEAR SPECIAL PAMPHLET

First published in 2017
by Eyewear Publishing Ltd
Suite 333, 19-21 Crawford Street
Marylebone, London W1H 1PJ
United Kingdom

Typeset with graphic design by Edwin Smet
Author photo by Ester Dewey
Printed in England by Lightning Source

ISBN 978-1-911335-85-6

Eyewear wishes to thank Jonathan Wonham for his generous patronage of our press.

WWW.EYEWEARPUBLISHING.COM

For my mum

TABLE OF CONTENTS

9 HOTEL BRAVO

10 JESSICA JONES

11 TOP DECK OF THE BUS

12 'ARE YOU HERE WITH BOBBY?'

13 A PORTRAIT OF THE ARTIST AS A YOUNG WOMAN

14 THE TWO BARS OUTSIDE EUSTON STATION

15 FLATMATES

16 FLIES

17 VALENTINE'S DAY

18 MOLES

19 HUNGER

20 LADY ON THE UNDERGROUND

21 MY BOYFRIEND'S IN LOVE WITH JEREMY CORBYN

22 MOTHER'S DAY

24 SORRY, MUM

25 SORRY, BABY

26 MOSQUITOES

27 SEWING MACHINE

28 GATO

29 I AM VERY GRATEFUL FOR CITALOPRAM

30 MAMMOTH IN LISBON

31 HEMLOCK

32 BODILY FICTIONS

34 ACKNOWLEDGEMENTS

HOTEL BRAVO

'All property is theft!'
you shout from the rooftop of the warehouse,
like Malcolm McDowell but without the rifle
with which to gun down your authority figures.

Later on the turntable
we play Sinatra,
each thinking about his love for Ava Gardner
from opposite sides of the room.

You think you've been bitten by a bedbug
so we turn the mattress
and cover ourselves and the cat
in diatomaceous earth

while Frank sings about the wee small hours.
We're living them from bed
and the morning won't be morning
just last night's takeaway

ordered after the supermarkets closed,
credit card between your teeth,
NATO-ising your postcode.
We're living in the Hotel Bravo.

JESSICA JONES

Gulp down another whiskey, Jessica.
It's OK to be an icon to moody teenagers
in leather jackets all across America.
They are not as beautiful, but their rage's
out in the pout of your bee-stung lips
and the gloaming of your hair against
a pinkly fresh-slapped cheek. Conscript
us in the war to make a kind of sense
of locking a woman up to make her smile.
When every domestic drama's
televised to make it worth our while,
maybe we all have a kind of trauma.
Your ex-boyfriend is everyone's ex-boyfriend.
Not everybody has a bulletproof bartender.

TOP DECK OF THE BUS

At closing time, you leave me on the street
to go to Tesco, but I know a sausage roll
won't forgive you or press its processed meat
heart into your hands before you eat it whole.
No matter how many times you see me
to the bus but not my door, I'll always
sit at the front of the top deck and plea
with the streetlights that it'll happen one day,
that you won't check your phone while I'm in the loo
then show me the girl you matched with,
that I'll tell you I'm in love with you
at long last, hopeless, hopelessly, at which
you won't look into your can of Carling:
'All the more fool both of us, darling.'

'ARE YOU HERE WITH BOBBY?'

Reads the graffiti on the door
of the toilet I'm currently leaning over.

'Yeah, he used to say beautiful things to me too.'
The marker is faded

as if Bobby is a ghost,
some ectoplasmic fuckboy, tethered

to the wanton grief of a girl
in such torment from a random transgression

that she wrote his name on the door of a pisser.
I'm not here with Bobby,

but I'd like someone to say something beautiful to me,
even if it's just the liquor.

A PORTRAIT OF THE ARTIST AS A YOUNG WOMAN

She probably works in a pub,
covering up despite the heat
in case an unwelcome comment is invited.
That said, she probably enjoys
tempting fate and making a joke
whenever someone orders a Longhorn.
She probably writes small poems
about her small world
because she can't afford much else.

THE TWO BARS OUTSIDE EUSTON STATION

The bus parts the sea
of happy hour worshippers,
the two bars outside Euston station
speckled with white, pink and blue collars,
rolled up shirtsleeves in the heat.
I imagine the men as two armies of Middle Earth,
the bars towering above like pinnacles of achievement,
or as the Sharks and Jets,
poised to break into song at any moment.
With soundless laughter,
the hive are drowning
in another nectar's sap.

FLATMATES

Gather, sisters
in our ex-council house
on the estate.
There's a weird prison-like bit
like where they used to keep the drunks,
where we howl at the moon
and perform heathen rituals
with tinnies and new music videos.
We pray to the universe
invariably to let it all end, or
please please please
to let us get what we want, one day.
What magical arrogance,
our little damp nirvana
at the centre of a world that spins so fast.

FLIES

I am sharing my room with four of them,
synchronised swimmers in the air's ocean.
My cat and I watch from the bed.

Tiny astronauts in a cosmos
that smells like lavender incense,
they are here to gather data,

to figure out if there's life
among the pizza boxes and general detritus
of a woman in her twenties.

The cat swings round to squint at me
and I wonder if the problem is the unrefreshed litter box.
Tracey Emin, go fuck yourself.

VALENTINE'S DAY

A glass of wine in a bookshop,
Emily Dickinson's envelope poems
and Hegelian Marxism
in the shape of Slavoj Žižek.

In the middle, a Venn diagram
of all the differences between us.
Still, we are alone at the table,
giggling like teenagers.

Later I get the phone call:
'Are you home, can you talk?'
Never a precursor to good news.
While I've been growing an eternity

she's been cultivating clouds
in her mammary glands.
'It's not dangerous, I promise,'
but the red light's already behind us.

MOLES

Peppered with precious pockmarks
passed down from my mother,
little brown stars between which my skin
draws constellations.
From a special, select few
hairs grow, longer and darker than their downy cousins,
like palm trees in Hollywood.
I pick at them in attempts to erase
scabs under dermatillomaniac fingers,
burn them off with apple cider vinegar,
pluck each hair viciously on the tube,
even though that's supposed to give you cancer.
I imagine her dolled up in a scarf
like Jackie Kennedy with her beauty marks,
lounging in a garden with a mojito,
except now the taste of alcohol
makes her sick.

HUNGER

I keep an empty stomach
as empty as my mind,
like I've swallowed my thoughts,
paperweight moths
changeable as sheets
lights as whims.
I guess I'm trying to be the opposite
of her fecundity,
scared of my body being blighted
with anything else deathly.

LADY ON THE UNDERGROUND

Lady on the underground,
I like the way you've done your contour
and the way the fluoro light above your head
makes your cheekbones cut like insults.

I like your lovely boyfriend,
the way he sits, casually resting a wrist
on your thigh. I like your blue eyes,
peering through their own tunnels of smoky brown shadow.

I like your painted mouth, bloody
Cupid's bow puckered like a teardrop.
I like your high heels,
how they pick you up at the right stop.

You must be going to a very fancy party.
Careful not to fall over my multi-pack of toilet roll.

MY BOYFRIEND'S IN LOVE WITH JEREMY CORBYN

Hey Jeremy,
I don't know how you feel about polygamy

but you've been volunteered against your will
and shall be brought here to fulfil

the deepest, darkest desires of my boyfriend,
who, one evening a few weekends

ago, looked me in the eye
with a face like he might actually cry,

to tell me, 'I think I'm in love with Jeremy Corbyn.'
Now, he's not the first to have been

wooed by a righteously principled man.
He said, 'I think it's because he makes jam.'

So Jeremy, I'm afraid you two must be lovers
and whisper together about manhole covers.

MOTHER'S DAY

We went to see you in the hospital,
almost comically dopey and
tucked up like a child under paper covers.
We gave you the cards I went out and bought that morning
and tried to be cheerful, despite
the tubes and machines
adorning your wheeled bed like a halo,
the dreadful heat the doctors insisted
was necessary to prevent rejection
and the fact that at your feet
lay a plastic bag full of your shit.
They made us take our flowers
back out with us.
Something was beeping –
you'd knocked a cannula out of your hand
with a minor movement, scratching, or reaching for water –
the godlike machine protesting
for a nurse.
We, desperate, went to comfort it
but had no way to understand
the red light flashing above a green line's oscillation.
The surgery went well, you said,
you were glad it was all over,
though your tummy felt tight from the skin they took
and you were woken up every two hours in the night
so they could check that the new breast,
made from your belly fat,
was behaving as it should, or should not.
I think of the old flesh,
lumpy, disregarded,
translucent like a shrink-wrapped chicken in a supermarket.

I'd like to ask it
why it tried to kill my mother
making reproductions of her cells
when she's already got us.
I came with you to the appointment
when they did an ultrasound on your tummy
to look for the important blood vessels that mustn't be cut
and doodle on you like a whiteboard or a PETA advert.
We heard the blood whooshing,
whale song or something from another planet
only with a regular human heartbeat.
After the doctors left and you'd wiped off the medical goo,
gotten dressed and cried a bit,
you looked at me funny and said
'The last time someone did that, it was you'.

SORRY, MUM

The island floats
safe in amniotic fluid
clutching tight in an insisting fist
the last real lifeline.

Now I cling to a bottle
of wine and a cigarette,
still looking for an answer.
Sorry I yelled at you when you got cancer.

SORRY, BABY

Every day I take a pill
to trick my body.
A fake crusader, a diversion tactic, a car backfire
instead of a gunshot.

Kronos ate his children too,
I think, as I swallow the little spaceship whole,
my uterine lining preparing to worship the baby
that effervesces in my gut.

MOSQUITOES

In Amsterdam,
we heard the whine
wheedling like a sycophant,
hands outstretched for praise.

Jewellery melting in the heat,
I said 'Fetch me the magazine,'
air thick with the expectation
of our first holiday without fighting.

We broke up in Berlin –
you walking twenty paces ahead,
me making a scene in a Greek restaurant,
our tragicomedy brought to life.

In Amsterdam,
I stalked our enemies and
swatted them,
staining the walls with your blood.

SEWING MACHINE

A five finger fillet dance
with a nimble needle,
you're staring at the fabric's edge
in a seamstress' trance.
I fetch a box from the cupboard.
It rattles at my touch,
and you say, 'Pick one'.
I remember them like a treasure horde,
the buttons, ancient coins
from some deep layer of the earth
sorted colour by colour
in compartments blue to bronze.
I used to sneak up on them,
run them through my fingers,
put their cool smoothness to my face,
to my mouth, under my tongue.
I swallowed one once
and had to hang my head
over the side of the bed
till it climbed back up my throat.
That was before the numbness,
and now they're just buttons.
I pick a small black one, humble,
like the kind from my school skirt.
You show me how to set up the machine,
hand me the seam ripper, we cut
the hole together, mark the place
and attach the button, stroke by stroke.
Two floating halves
put back together,
simple as that.

GATO

The cat sits
unattended on the chair.
An existential nightmare descends
like a catnip-filled banana toy on a string.
I wonder if I should give it some citalopram.

I'M VERY GRATEFUL FOR CITALOPRAM

Accompanied everywhere by the smell of sweat,
I am wet with it, almost enough to be done with it.
The slick that shines on my upper lip
might be enough to make me quit.

It even overpowers the biscuit-brown waft
of fake tan when I reach to grab the rail
on the tube. Sorry, fellow passengers,
it's just the stronger beating of my more-alive heart,
pushing the sweet sweat out.

Legs at night dance a tarantella,
won't let me sleep, there's a watch to keep.
Toe tapping with movements to make,
jaw grinding with things to say,
eyes filling with colour again.

When I call her, she says 'You sound well,'
and I say, 'Yeah, Mum, I'm doing good.
Today I remembered what it was like to feel bored.'
She says, 'That's wonderful, sweetheart,'
and I know she means it.
She hates my tattoos but she hates
my arms' other marks even more.

MAMMOTH IN LISBON

M is for massaman, for metastasise, for murder. The mammoth sits in thought, gentle-ended trunk at play with a splinter on the bench. Elsewhere upright shapes bask in the beat down of the sunshine, pink underbellies ripening with a lack of hair. M is for matted. Sweat slides down the mammoth's trunk, bullwhip tail hisses at flies. Lumbering, large, laborious. After all that ice, the heat is what the mammoth needs, the air around him vignetting with steam like an old film photograph. He will nestle here, growing secretly until discovered by a routine MRI. These new bald monkeys don't trouble him much. Perhaps he will take a stroll down to the watering hole, or while away an afternoon at chess. M is for maudlin, for missing, for malingerer.

HEMLOCK

Pristine in sleep
It is all I can do
Not to wake you

Feel the muscles in your back
Jump at my touch
The swaying sigh

Of your outwards inwards breath
Rolling toes
Arching spine

I finger the gaps in your vertebrae
Slot into your shadow
Like under a shop awning in the rain

Can I keep you like this?
Deathly darling no
Don't stir don't wake don't go

BODILY FICTIONS

each blink a comma

                in the sentence of the mouth

deep in the gut churns   the nauseating knowledge

                everything is not quite all right

the curves of hips a pair of parentheses

                the slope of shoulders
                a sensual semicolon

        tapping toe writes in Morse code

                on the bleached lino

a lick of the lips
to a lick of the fingers
        turn the page
            of the magazine in the waiting room

            every inhale the knock knock knock of an MRI
            every exhale the squeak of a shoe

torso
its peaks and valleys
like a mountain range
        full of waterfalls
            and death drops

what stories the body tells
        each tumour a cliffhanger

ACKNOWLEDGEMENTS

Thank you firstly and mostly to Todd Swift for his editorial wisdom and encouragement, and to Rosanna, Edwin, Oliver and Sarah at Eyewear.

Thank you Lily Newman, Lucas Grant, Ester Dewey, Fifi Dewey, Emma Smith and Dominique Eguren.

Thank you Dominic Hicks, unwitting muse.

Thanks also to Julie Jordan, Charlie Payne, and Ross Payne.